THE HARP-WEAVER
AND OTHER POEMS

THE HARP–WEAVER

AND

OTHER POEMS

BY

EDNA ST. VINCENT MILLAY

Publishers

HARPER & BROTHERS

NEW YORK AND LONDON

MCMXXIII

TO
MY MOTHER

CONTENTS

PART ONE

PART TWO

CONTENTS

viii

CONTENTS

PART FIVE

SONNETS FROM AN UNGRAFTED TREE

CONTENTS

PART ONE

MY HEART, BEING HUNGRY

My heart, being hungry, feeds on food
   The fat of heart despise.
Beauty where beauty never stood,
   And sweet where no sweet lies
I gather to my querulous need,
Having a growing heart to feed.

It may be, when my heart is dull,
   Having attained its girth,
I shall not find so beautiful
   The meagre shapes of earth,
Nor linger in the rain to mark
The smell of tansy through the dark.

AUTUMN CHANT

Now the autumn shudders
   In the rose's root.
Far and wide the ladders
   Lean among the fruit.

Now the autumn clambers
   Up the trellised frame,
And the rose remembers
   The dust from which it came.

Brighter than the blossom
   On the rose's bough
Sits the wizened, orange,
   Bitter berry now;

Beauty never slumbers;
   All is in her name;
But the rose remembers
   The dust from which it came.

NUIT BLANCHE

I AM a shepherd of those sheep
   That climb a wall by night,
One after one, until I sleep,
   Or the black pane goes white.
Because of which I cannot see
   A flock upon a hill,
But doubts come tittering up to me
   That should by day be still.
And childish griefs I have outgrown
   Into my eyes are thrust,
Till my dull tears go dropping down
   Like lead into the dust.

THREE SONGS FROM
"THE LAMP AND THE BELL"

I

Oh, little rose tree, bloom!
Summer is nearly over.
The dahlias bleed, and the phlox is seed.
Nothing's left of the clover.
And the path of the poppy no one knows.
I would blossom if I were a rose.

Summer, for all your guile,
Will brown in a week to Autumn,
And launched leaves throw a shadow below
Over the brook's clear bottom,—
And the chariest bud the year can boast
Be brought to bloom by the chastening frost.

II

Beat me a crown of bluer metal;
   Fret it with stones of a foreign style:
The heart grows weary after a little
   Of what it loved for a little while.

6

Weave me a robe of richer fibre;
    Pattern its web with a rare device.
Give away to the child of a neighbor
    This gold gown I was glad in twice.

But buy me a singer to sing one song—
    Song about nothing—song about sheep—
Over and over, all day long;
    Patch me again my thread-bare sleep.

III

Rain comes down
And hushes the town.
And where is the voice that I heard crying?

Snow settles
Over the nettles.
Where is the voice that I heard crying?

Sand at last
On the drifting mast.
And where is the voice that I heard crying?

Earth now
On the busy brow.
And where is the voice that I heard crying?

7

THE WOOD ROAD

IF I were to walk this way
   Hand in hand with Grief,
I should mark that maple-spray
   Coming into leaf.
I should note how the old burrs
   Rot upon the ground.
Yes, though Grief should know me hers
   While the world goes round,
It could not in truth be said
   This was lost on me:
A rock-maple showing red,
   Burrs beneath a tree.

FEAST

I DRANK at every vine.
  The last was like the first.
I came upon no wine
  So wonderful as thirst.

I gnawed at every root.
  I ate of every plant.
I came upon no fruit
  So wonderful as want.

Feed the grape and bean
  To the vintner and monger;
I will lie down lean
  With my thirst and my hunger.

SOUVENIR

Just a rainy day or two
In a windy tower,
That was all I had of you—
Saving half an hour

Marred by greeting passing groups
In a cinder walk,
Near some naked blackberry hoops
Dim with purple chalk.

I remember three or four
Things you said in spite,
And an ugly coat you wore,
Plaided black and white.

Just a rainy day or two
And a bitter word.
Why do I remember you
As a singing bird?

SCRUB

If I grow bitterly,
Like a gnarled and stunted tree,
Bearing harshly of my youth
Puckered fruit that sears the mouth;
If I make of my drawn boughs
An inhospitable house,
Out of which I never pry
Towards the water and the sky,
Under which I stand and hide
And hear the day go by outside;
It is that a wind too strong
Bent my back when I was young,
It is that I fear the rain
Lest it blister me again.

THE GOOSE-GIRL

SPRING rides no horses down the hill,
But comes on foot, a goose-girl still.
And all the loveliest things there be
Come simply, so, it seems to me.
If ever I said, in grief or pride,
I tired of honest things, I lied;
And should be cursed forevermore
With Love in laces, like a whore,
And neighbors cold, and friends unsteady,
And Spring on horseback, like a lady!

THE DRAGONFLY

I WOUND myself in a white cocoon of singing,
  All day long in the brook's uneven bed,
  Measuring out my soul in a mucous thread;
Dimly now to the brook's green bottom clinging,
  Men behold me, a worm spun-out and dead,
Walled in an iron house of silky singing.

Nevertheless at length, O reedy shallows,
  Not as a plodding nose to the slimy stem,
  But as a brazen wing with a spangled hem,
Over the jewel-weed and the pink marshmallows,
  Free of these and making a song of them,
I shall arise, and a song of the reedy shallows!

PART TWO

DEPARTURE

It's little I care what path I take,
And where it leads it's little I care;
But out of this house, lest my heart break,
I must go, and off somewhere.

It's little I know what's in my heart,
What's in my mind it's little I know,
But there's that in me must up and start,
And it's little I care where my feet go.

I wish I could walk for a day and a night,
And find me at dawn in a desolate place
With never the rut of a road in sight,
Nor the roof of a house, nor the eyes of a face.

I wish I could walk till my blood should spout,
And drop me, never to stir again,
On a shore that is wide, for the tide is out,
And the weedy rocks are bare to the rain.

But dump or dock, where the path I take
Brings up, it's little enough I care;
And it's little I'd mind the fuss they'll make,
Huddled dead in a ditch somewhere.

"Is something the matter, dear," she said,
"That you sit at your work so silently?"
"No, mother, no, 'twas a knot in my thread.
There goes the kettle, I'll make the tea."

THE RETURN FROM TOWN

As I sat down by Saddle Stream
　　To bathe my dusty feet there,
A boy was standing on the bridge
　　Any girl would meet there.

As I went over Woody Knob
　　And dipped into the hollow,
A youth was coming up the hill
　　Any maid would follow.

Then in I turned at my own gate,—
　　And nothing to be sad for—
To such a man as any wife
　　Would pass a pretty lad for.

A VISIT TO THE ASYLUM

ONCE from a big, big building,
When I was small, small,
The queer folk in the windows
Would smile at me and call.

And in the hard wee gardens
Such pleasant men would hoe:
"Sir, may we touch the little girl's hair?"—
It was so red, you know.

They cut me colored asters
With shears so sharp and neat,
They brought me grapes and plums and pears
And pretty cakes to eat.

And out of all the windows,
No matter where we went,
The merriest eyes would follow me
And make me compliment

There were a thousand windows,
All latticed up and down.
And up to all the windows,
When we went back to town,

The queer folk put their faces,
As gentle as could be;
"Come again, little girl!" they called, and I
Called back, "You come see me!"

THE SPRING AND THE FALL

IN the spring of the year, in the spring of the year,
I walked the road beside my dear.
The trees were black where the bark was wet.
I see them yet, in the spring of the year.
He broke me a bough of the blossoming peach
That was out of the way and hard to reach.

In the fall of the year, in the fall of the year,
I walked the road beside my dear.
The rooks went up with a raucous trill.
I hear them still, in the fall of the year.
He laughed at all I dared to praise,
And broke my heart, in little ways.

Year be springing or year be falling,
The bark will drip and the birds be calling.
There's much that's fine to see and hear
In the spring of a year, in the fall of a year.
'Tis not love's going hurts my days,
But that it went in little ways.

THE CURSE

Oh, lay my ashes on the wind
That blows across the sea.
And I shall meet a fisherman
Out of Capri,

And he will say, seeing me,
"What a strange thing!
Like a fish's scale or a
Butterfly's wing."

Oh, lay my ashes on the wind
That blows away the fog.
And I shall meet a farmer boy
Leaping through the bog,

And he will say, seeing me,
"What a strange thing!
Like a peat-ash or a
Butterfly's wing."

And I shall blow to your house
And, sucked against the pane,
See you take your sewing up
And lay it down again.

And you will say, seeing me,
"What a strange thing!
Like a plum petal or a
Butterfly's wing."

And none at all will know me
That knew me well before.
But I will settle at the root
That climbs about your door,

And fishermen and farmers
May see me and forget,
But I'll be a bitter berry
In your brewing yet.

KEEN

WEEP him dead and mourn as you may,
    Me, I sing as I must:
Blessed be Death, that cuts in marble
    What would have sunk to dust!

Blessed be Death, that took my love
    And buried him in the sea,
Where never a lie nor a bitter word
    Will out of his mouth at me.

This I have to hold to my heart,
    This to take by the hand:
Sweet we were for a summer month
    As the sun on the dry white sand;

Mild we were for a summer month
    As the wind from over the weirs.
And blessed be Death, that hushed with salt
    The harsh and slovenly years!

Who builds her a house with love for timber
    Builds her a house of foam.
And I'd rather be bride to a lad gone down
    Than widow to one safe home.

THE BETROTHAL

Oh, come, my lad, or go, my lad,
And love me if you like.
I shall not hear the door shut
Nor the knocker strike.

Oh, bring me gifts or beg me gifts,
And wed me if you will.
I'd make a man a good wife,
Sensible and still.

And why should I be cold, my lad,
And why should you repine,
Because I love a dark head
That never will be mine?

I might as well be easing you
As lie alone in bed
And waste the night in wanting
A cruel dark head.

You might as well be calling yours
What never will be his,
And one of us be happy.
There's few enough as is.

26

HUMORESQUE

"Heaven bless the babe!" they said.
"What queer books she must have read!"
(Love, by whom I was beguiled,
Grant I may not bear a child.)

"Little does she guess to-day
What the world may be!" they say.
(Snow, drift deep and cover
Till the spring my murdered lover.)

THE POND

In this pond of placid water,
 Half a hundred years ago,
So they say, a farmer's daughter,
 Jilted by her farmer beau,

Waded out among the rushes,
 Scattering the blue dragon-flies;
That dried stick the ripple washes
 Marks the spot, I should surmise.

Think, so near the public highway,
 Well frequented even then!
Can you not conceive the sly way,—
 Hearing wheels or seeing men

Passing on the road above,—
 With a gesture feigned and silly,
Ere she drowned herself for love,
 She would reach to pluck a lily?

THE BALLAD OF THE HARP-WEAVER

"Son," said my mother,
  When I was knee-high,
"You've need of clothes to cover you,
  And not a rag have I.

"There's nothing in the house
  To make a boy breeches,
Nor shears to cut a cloth with
  Nor thread to take stitches.

"There's nothing in the house
  But a loaf-end of rye,
And a harp with a woman's head
  Nobody will buy,"
  And she began to cry.

That was in the early fall.
  When came the late fall,
"Son," she said, "the sight of you
  Makes your mother's blood crawl,—

"Little skinny shoulder-blades
  Sticking through your clothes!
And where you'll get a jacket from
  God above knows.

"It's lucky for me, lad,
  Your daddy's in the ground,
And can't see the way I let
  His son go around!"
  And she made a queer sound.

That was in the late fall.
  When the winter came,
I'd not a pair of breeches
  Nor a shirt to my name.

I couldn't go to school,
  Or out of doors to play.
And all the other little boys
  Passed our way.

"Son," said my mother,
  "Come, climb into my lap,
And I'll chafe your little bones
  While you take a nap."

30

And, oh, but we were silly
  For half an hour or more,
Me with my long legs
  Dragging on the floor,

A-rock-rock-rocking
  To a mother-goose rhyme!
Oh, but we were happy
  For half an hour's time!

But there was I, a great boy,
  And what would folks say
To hear my mother singing me
  To sleep all day,
  In such a daft way?

Men say the winter
  Was bad that year;
Fuel was scarce,
  And food was dear.

A wind with a wolf's head
  Howled about our door,
And we burned up the chairs
  And sat upon the floor.

All that was left us
  Was a chair we couldn't break,
And the harp with a woman's head
  Nobody would take,
  For song or pity's sake.

The night before Christmas
  I cried with the cold,
I cried myself to sleep
  Like a two-year-old.

And in the deep night
  I felt my mother rise,
And stare down upon me
  With love in her eyes.

I saw my mother sitting
  On the one good chair,
A light falling on her
  From I couldn't tell where,

Looking nineteen,
  And not a day older,
And the harp with a woman's head
  Leaned against her shoulder.

Her thin fingers, moving
  In the thin, tall strings,
Were weav-weav-weaving
  Wonderful things.

Many bright threads,
  From where I couldn't see,
Were running through the harp-strings
  Rapidly,

And gold threads whistling
  Through my mother's hand.
I saw the web grow,
  And the pattern expand.

She wove a child's jacket,
  And when it was done
She laid it on the floor
  And wove another one.

She wove a red cloak
  So regal to see,
"She's made it for a king's son,"
  I said, "and not for me."
  But I knew it was for me.

33

She wove a pair of breeches
  Quicker than that!
She wove a pair of boots
  And a little cocked hat.

She wove a pair of mittens,
  She wove a little blouse,
She wove all night
  In the still, cold house.

She sang as she worked,
  And the harp-strings spoke;
Her voice never faltered,
  And the thread never broke.
  And when I awoke,—

There sat my mother
  With the harp against her shoulder,
Looking nineteen
  And not a day older,

A smile about her lips,
  And a light about her head,
And her hands in the harp-strings
  Frozen dead.

34

And piled up beside her
  And toppling to the skies,
Were the clothes of a king's son,
  Just my size.

PART THREE

NEVER MAY THE FRUIT BE PLUCKED

Never, never may the fruit be plucked from the bough
And gathered into barrels.
He that would eat of love must eat it where it hangs.
Though the branches bend like reeds,
Though the ripe fruit splash in the grass or wrinkle
    on the tree,
He that would eat of love may bear away with him
Only what his belly can hold,
Nothing in the apron,
Nothing in the pockets.
Never, never may the fruit be gathered from the bough
And harvested in barrels.
The winter of love is a cellar of empty bins,
In an orchard soft with rot.

THE CONCERT

No, I will go alone.
I will come back when it's over.
Yes, of course I love you.
No, it will not be long.
Why may you not come with me?—
You are too much my lover.
You would put yourself
Between me and song.

If I go alone,
Quiet and suavely clothed,
My body will die in its chair,
And over my head a flame,
A mind that is twice my own,
Will mark with icy mirth
The wise advance and retreat
Of armies without a country,
Storming a nameless gate,
Hurling terrible javelins down
From the shouting walls of a singing town
Where no women wait!

Armies clean of love and hate,
Marching lines of pitiless sound
Climbing hills to the sun and hurling
Golden spears to the ground!
Up the lines a silver runner
Bearing a banner whereon is scored
The milk and steel of a bloodless wound
Healed at length by the sword!

You and I have nothing to do with music.
We may not make of music a filigree frame,
Within which you and I,
Tenderly glad we came,
Sit smiling, hand in hand.

Come now, be content.
I will come back to you, I swear I will;
And you will know me still.
I shall be only a little taller
Than when I went.

HYACINTH

I AM in love with him to whom a hyacinth is dearer
Than I shall ever be dear.
On nights when the field-mice are abroad he cannot
sleep:
He hears their narrow teeth at the bulbs of his
hyacinths.
But the gnawing at my heart he does not hear.

TO ONE WHO MIGHT HAVE BORNE
A MESSAGE

Had I known that you were going
I would have given you messages for her,
Now two years dead,
Whom I shall always love.

As it is, should she entreat you how it goes with
     me,
You must reply, as well as with most, you fancy;
That I love easily, and pass the time.
And she will not know how all day long between
My life and me her shadow intervenes,
A young thin girl,
Wearing a white skirt and a purple sweater
And a narrow pale blue ribbon about her hair.

I used to say to her, "I love you
Because your face is such a pretty color,
No other reason."
But it was not true.

Oh, had I only known that you were going,
I could have given you messages for her!

SIEGE

THIS I do, being mad:
Gather baubles about me,
Sit in a circle of toys, and all the time
Death beating the door in.

White jade and an orange pitcher,
Hindu idol, Chinese god,—
Maybe next year, when I'm richer—
Carved beads and a lotus pod. . . .

And all this time
Death beating the door in.

THE CAIRN

WHEN I think of the little children learning
In all the schools of the world,
Learning in Danish, learning in Japanese
That two and two are four, and where the rivers of
　　the world
Rise, and the names of the mountains and the principal
　　cities,
My heart breaks.
Come up, children! Toss your little stones gaily
On the great cairn of Knowledge!
(Where lies what Euclid knew, a little gray stone,
What Plato, what Pascal, what Galileo:
Little gray stones, little gray stones on a cairn.)
Tell me, what is the name of the highest mountain?
Name me a crater of fire! a peak of snow!
Name me the mountains on the moon!
But the name of the mountain that you climb all day,
Ask not your teacher that.

SPRING SONG

I KNOW why the yellow forsythia
Holds its breath and will not bloom,
And the robin thrusts his beak in his wing.

Want me to tell you?   Think you can bear it?
Cover your eyes with your hand and hear it.
You know how cold the days are still?
And everybody saying how late the Spring is?
Well—cover your eyes with your hand—the
     thing is,
There isn't going to be any Spring.

No parking here!   No parking here!
They said to Spring: No parking here!

Spring came on as she always does,
Laid her hand on the yellow forsythia,—
Little boys turned in their sleep and smiled,
Dreaming of marbles, dreaming of agates;
Little girls leapt from their beds to see
Spring come by with her painted wagons,
Colored wagons creaking with wonder—

Laid her hand on the robin's throat;
When up comes you-know-who, my dear,
You-know-who in a fine blue coat,
And says to Spring: No parking here!

No parking here!   No parking here!
Move on!   Move on!   No parking here!

Come walk with me in the city gardens.
(Better keep an eye out for you-know-who)
Did ever you see such a sickly showing?—
Middle of June, and nothing growing;
The gardeners peer and scratch their heads
And drop their sweat on the tulip-beds,
But not a blade thrusts through.

Come, move on!   Don't you know how to walk?
No parking here!   And no back-talk!

Oh, well,—hell, it's all for the best.
She certainly made a lot of clutter,
Dropping petals under the trees,
Taking your mind off your bread and butter.

Anyhow, it's nothing to me.
I can remember, and so can you.
(Though we'd better watch out for you-know-
 who,
When we sit around remembering Spring).

We shall hardly notice in a year or two.
You can get accustomed to anything.

MEMORY OF CAPE COD

THE wind in the ash-tree sounds like surf on the shore
　　at Truro.
I will shut my eyes . . . hush, be still with your silly
　　bleating, sheep on Shillingstone Hill . . .

They said: Come along! They said: Leave your
　　pebbles on the sand and come along, it's long after
　　sunset!
The mosquitoes will be thick in the pine-woods along
　　by Long Nook, the wind's died down!
They said: Leave your pebbles on the sand, and your
　　shells, too, and come along, we'll find you another
　　beach like the beach at Truro.

Let me listen to wind in the ash . . . it sounds like
　　surf on the shore.

PART FOUR

SONNETS

I

WHEN you, that at this moment are to me
Dearer than words on paper, shall depart,
And be no more the warder of my heart,
Whereof again myself shall hold the key;
And be no more—what now you seem to be—
The sun, from which all excellences start
In a round nimbus, nor a broken dart
Of moonlight, even, splintered on the sea;
I shall remember only of this hour—
And weep somewhat, as now you see me weep—
The pathos of your love, that, like a flower,
Fearful of death yet amorous of sleep,
Droops for a moment and beholds, dismayed,
The wind whereon its petals shall be laid.

II

THAT Love at length should find me out and bring
This fierce and trivial brow unto the dust,
Is, after all, I must confess, but just;
There is a subtle beauty in this thing,
A wry perfection; wherefore now let sing
All voices how into my throat is thrust,
Unwelcome as Death's own, Love's bitter crust,
All criers proclaim it, and all steeples ring.
This being done, there let the matter rest.
What more remains is neither here nor there.
That you requite me not is plain to see;
Myself your slave herein have I confessed:
Thus far, indeed, the world may mock at me;
But if I suffer, it is my own affair.

III

Love is not blind. I see with single eye
Your ugliness and other women's grace.
I know the imperfection of your face,—
The eyes too wide apart, the brow too high
For beauty. Learned from earliest youth am I
In loveliness, and cannot so erase
Its letters from my mind, that I may trace
You faultless, I must love until I die.
More subtle is the sovereignty of love:
So am I caught that when I say, "Not fair,"
'Tis but as if I said, "Not here—not there—
Not risen—not writing letters." Well I know
What is this beauty men are babbling of;
I wonder only why they prize it so.

IV

I KNOW I am but summer to your heart,
And not the full four seasons of the year;
And you must welcome from another part
Such noble moods as are not mine, my dear.
No gracious weight of golden fruits to sell
Have I, nor any wise and wintry thing;
And I have loved you all too long and well
To carry still the high sweet breast of Spring.
Wherefore I say: O love, as summer goes,
I must be gone, steal forth with silent drums,
That you may hail anew the bird and rose
When I come back to you, as summer comes.
Else will you seek, at some not distant time,
Even your summer in another clime.

V

I PRAY you if you love me, bear my joy
A little while, or let me weep your tears;
I, too, have seen the quavering Fate destroy
Your destiny's bright spinning—the dull shears
Meeting not neatly, chewing at the thread,—
Nor can you well be less aware how fine,
How staunch as wire, and how unwarranted
Endures the golden fortune that is mine.
I pray you for this day at least, my dear,
Fare by my side, that journey in the sun;
Else must I turn me from the blossoming year
And walk in grief the way that you have gone.
Let us go forth together to the spring:
Love must be this, if it be anything.

VI

Pity me not because the light of day
At close of day no longer walks the sky;
Pity me not for beauties passed away
From field and thicket as the year goes by;
Pity me not the waning of the moon,
Nor that the ebbing tide goes out to sea,
Nor that a man's desire is hushed so soon,
And you no longer look with love on me.
This have I known always: Love is no more
Than the wide blossom which the wind assails,
Than the great tide that treads the shifting shore,
Strewing fresh wreckage gathered in the gales;
Pity me that the heart is slow to learn
What the swift mind beholds at every turn.

IX

HERE is a wound that never will heal, I know,
Being wrought not of a dearness and a death,
But of a love turned ashes and the breath
Gone out of beauty; never again will grow
The grass on that scarred acre, though I sow
Young seed there yearly and the sky bequeath
Its friendly weathers down, far underneath
Shall be such bitterness of an old woe.
That April should be shattered by a gust,
That August should be levelled by a rain,
I can endure, and that the lifted dust
Of man should settle to the earth again;
But that a dream can die, will be a thrust
Between my ribs forever of hot pain.

X

I SHALL go back again to the bleak shore
And build a little shanty on the sand,
In such a way that the extremest band
Of brittle seaweed will escape my door
But by a yard or two; and nevermore
Shall I return to take you by the hand;
I shall be gone to what I understand,
And happier than I ever was before.
The love that stood a moment in your eyes,
The words that lay a moment on your tongue,
Are one with all that in a moment dies,
A little under-said and over-sung.
But I shall find the sullen rocks and skies
Unchanged from what they were when I was
    young.

XI

Say what you will, and scratch my heart to find
The roots of last year's roses in my breast;
I am as surely riper in my mind
As if the fruit stood in the stalls confessed.
Laugh at the unshed leaf, say what you will,
Call me in all things what I was before,
A flutterer in the wind, a woman still;
I tell you I am what I was and more.
My branches weigh me down, frost cleans the air,
My sky is black with small birds bearing south;
Say what you will, confuse me with fine care,
Put by my word as but an April truth—
Autumn is no less on me that a rose
Hugs the brown bough and sighs before it goes.

XII

WHAT'S this of death, from you who never will
    die?
Think you the wrist that fashioned you in clay,
The thumb that set the hollow just that way
In your full throat and lidded the long eye
So roundly from the forehead, will let lie
Broken, forgotten, under foot some day
Your unimpeachable body, and so slay
The work he most had been remembered by?
I tell you this: whatever of dust to dust
Goes down, whatever of ashes may return
To its essential self in its own season,
Loveliness such as yours will not be lost,
But, cast in bronze upon his very urn,
Make known him Master, and for what good
    reason.

XIII

I SEE so clearly now my similar years
Repeat each other, shod in rusty black,
Like one hack following another hack
In meaningless procession, dry of tears,
Driven empty, lest the noses sharp as shears
Of gutter-urchins at a hearse's back
Should sniff a man died friendless, and attack
With silly scorn his deaf triumphant ears;
I see so clearly how my life must run
One year behind another year until
At length these bones that leap into the sun
Are lowered into the gravel, and lie still,
I would at times the funeral were done
And I abandoned on the ultimate hill.

XIV

YOUR face is like a chamber where a king
Dies of his wounds, untended and alone,
Stifling with courteous gesture the crude moan
That speaks too loud of mortal perishing,
Rising on elbow in the dark to sing
Some rhyme now out of season but well known
In days when banners in his face were blown
And every woman had a rose to fling.
I know that through your eyes which look on me
Who stand regarding you with pitiful breath,
You see beyond the moment's pause, you see
The sunny sky, the skimming bird beneath,
And, fronting on your windows hopelessly,
Black in the noon, the broad estates of Death.

XV

THE light comes back with Columbine; she brings
A touch of this, a little touch of that,
Coloured confetti, and a favour hat,
Patches, and powder, dolls that work by strings
And moons that work by switches, all the things
That please a sick man's fancy, and a flat
Spry convalescent kiss, and a small pat
Upon the pillow,—paper offerings.
The light goes out with her; the shadows sprawl.
Where she has left her fragrance like a shawl
I lie alone and pluck the counterpane,
Or on a dizzy elbow rise and hark—
And down like dominoes along the dark
Her little silly laughter spills again!

XVI

Lord Archer, Death, whom sent you in your
    stead?
What faltering prentice fumbled at your bow,
That now should wander with the insanguine dead
In whom forever the bright blood must flow?
Or is it rather that impairing Time
Renders yourself so random, or so dim?
Or are you sick of shadows and would climb
A while to light, a while detaining him?
For know, this was no mortal youth, to be
Of you confounded, but a heavenly guest,
Assuming earthly garb for love of me,
And hell's demure attire for love of jest:
Bringing me asphodel and a dark feather,
He will return, and we shall laugh together!

XVII

Loving you less than life, a little less
Than bitter-sweet upon a broken wall
Or bush-wood smoke in autumn, I confess
I cannot swear I love you not at all.
For there is that about you in this light—
A yellow darkness, sinister of rain—
Which sturdily recalls my stubborn sight
To dwell on you, and dwell on you again.
And I am made aware of many a week
I shall consume, remembering in what way
Your brown hair grows about your brow and
    cheek,
And what divine absurdities you say:
Till all the world, and I, and surely you,
Will know I love you, whether or not I do.

XVIII

I, BEING born a woman and distressed
By all the needs and notions of my kind,
Am urged by your propinquity to find
Your person fair, and feel a certain zest
To bear your body's weight upon my breast:
So subtly is the fume of life designed,
To clarify the pulse and cloud the mind,
And leave me once again undone, possessed.
Think not for this, however, the poor treason
Of my stout blood against my staggering brain,
I shall remember you with love, or season
My scorn with pity,—let me make it plain:
I find this frenzy insufficient reason
For conversation when we meet again.

XIX

WHAT lips my lips have kissed, and where, and
    why,
I have forgotten, and what arms have lain
Under my head till morning; but the rain
Is full of ghosts to-night, that tap and sigh
Upon the glass and listen for reply,
And in my heart there stirs a quiet pain
For unremembered lads that not again
Will turn to me at midnight with a cry.
Thus in the winter stands the lonely tree,
Nor knows what birds have vanished one by one,
Yet knows its boughs more silent than before:
I cannot say what loves have come and gone,
I only know that summer sang in me
A little while, that in me sings no more.

XX

Still will I harvest beauty where it grows:
In coloured fungus and the spotted fog
Surprised on foods forgotten; in ditch and bog
Filmed brilliant with irregular rainbows
Of rust and oil, where half a city throws
Its empty tins; and in some spongy log
Whence headlong leaps the oozy emerald
    frog. . . .
And a black pupil in the green scum shows.
Her the inhabiter of divers places
Surmising at all doors, I push them all.
Oh, you that fearful of a creaking hinge
Turn back forevermore with craven faces,
I tell you Beauty bears an ultra fringe
Unguessed of you upon her gossamer shawl!

XXI

How healthily their feet upon the floor
Strike down! These are no spirits, but a band
Of children, surely, leaping hand in hand
Into the air in groups of three and four,
Wearing their silken rags as if they wore
Leaves only and light grasses, or a strand
Of black elusive seaweed oozing sand,
And running hard as if along a shore.
I know how lost forever, and at length
How still these lovely tossing limbs shall lie,
And the bright laughter and the panting breath;
And yet, before such beauty and such strength,
Once more, as always when the dance is high,
I am rebuked that I believe in death.

XXII

Euclid alone has looked on Beauty bare.
Let all who prate of Beauty hold their peace,
And lay them prone upon the earth and cease
To ponder on themselves, the while they stare
At nothing, intricately drawn nowhere
In shapes of shifting lineage; let geese
Gabble and hiss, but heroes seek release
From dusty bondage into luminous air.
O blinding hour, O holy, terrible day,
When first the shaft into his vision shone
Of light anatomized!   Euclid alone
Has looked on Beauty bare.   Fortunate they
Who, though once only and then but far away,
Have heard her massive sandal set on stone.

PART FIVE

SONNETS FROM
AN UNGRAFTED TREE

SONNETS FROM AN UNGRAFTED TREE

I

So she came back into his house again
And watched beside his bed until he died,
Loving him not at all.   The winter rain
Splashed in the painted butter-tub outside,
Where once her red geraniums had stood,
Where still their rotted stalks were to be seen;
The thin log snapped; and she went out for wood,
Bareheaded, running the few steps between
The house and shed; there, from the sodden eaves
Blown back and forth on ragged ends of twine,
Saw the dejected creeping-jinny vine,
(And one, big-aproned, blithe, with stiff blue sleeves
Rolled to the shoulder that warm day in spring,
Who planted seeds, musing ahead to their far blos-
        soming).

II

THE last white sawdust on the floor was grown
Gray as the first, so long had he been ill;
The axe was nodding in the block; fresh-blown
And foreign came the rain across the sill,
But on the roof so steadily it drummed
She could not think a time it might not be—
In hazy summer, when the hot air hummed
With mowing, and locusts rising raspingly,
When that small bird with iridescent wings
And long incredible sudden silver tongue
Had just flashed (and yet may be not!) among
The dwarf nasturtiums—when no sagging springs
Of shower were in the whole bright sky, somehow
Upon this roof the rain would drum as it was drum-
    ming now.

III

SHE filled her arms with wood, and set her chin
Forward, to hold the highest stick in place,
No less afraid than she had always been
Of spiders up her arms and on her face,
But too impatient for a careful search
Or a less heavy loading, from the heap
Selecting hastily small sticks of birch,
For their curled bark, that instantly will leap
Into a blaze, nor thinking to return
Some day, distracted, as of old, to find
Smooth, heavy, round, green logs with a wet, gray rind
Only, and knotty chunks that will not burn,
(That day when dust is on the wood-box floor,
And some old catalogue, and a brown, shriveled apple
    core).

IV

THE white bark writhed and sputtered like a fish
Upon the coals, exuding odorous smoke.
She knelt and blew, in a surging desolate wish
For comfort; and the sleeping ashes woke
And scattered to the hearth, but no thin fire
Broke suddenly, the wood was wet with rain.
Then, softly stepping forth from her desire,
(Being mindful of like passion hurled in vain
Upon a similar task, in other days)
She thrust her breath against the stubborn coal,
Bringing to bear upon its hilt the whole
Of her still body . . . there sprang a little blaze . . .
A pack of hounds, the flame swept up the flue!—
And the blue night stood flattened against the window,
    staring through.

V

A wagon stopped before the house; she heard
The heavy oilskins of the grocer's man
Slapping against his legs. Of a sudden whirred
Her heart like a frightened partridge, and she ran
And slid the bolt, leaving his entrance free;
Then in the cellar way till he was gone
Hid, breathless, praying that he might not see
The chair sway she had laid her hand upon
In passing. Sour and damp from that dark vault
Arose to her the well-remembered chill;
She saw the narrow wooden stairway still
Plunging into the earth, and the thin salt
Crusting the crocks; until she knew him far,
So stood, with listening eyes upon the empty dough-
    nut jar.

VI

THEN cautiously she pushed the cellar door
And stepped into the kitchen—saw the track
Of muddy rubber boots across the floor,
The many paper parcels in a stack
Upon the dresser; with accustomed care
Removed the twine and put the wrappings by,
Folded, and the bags flat, that with an air
Of ease had been whipped open skillfully,
To the gape of children.   Treacherously dear
And simple was the dull, familiar task.
And so it was she came at length to ask:
How came the soda there?   The sugar here?
Then the dream broke.   Silent, she brought the mop,
And forced the trade-slip on the nail that held his
    razor strop.

VII

ONE way there was of muting in the mind
A little while the ever-clamorous care;
And there was rapture, of a decent kind,
In making mean and ugly objects fair:
Soft-sooted kettle-bottoms, that had been
Time after time set in above the fire,
Faucets, and candlesticks, corroded green,
To mine again from quarry; to attire
The shelves in paper petticoats, and tack
New oilcloth in the ringed-and-rotten's place,
Polish the stove till you could see your face,
And after nightfall rear an aching back
In a changed kitchen, bright as a new pin,
An advertisement, far too fine to cook a supper in.

VIII

SHE let them leave their jellies at the door
And go away, reluctant, down the walk.
She heard them talking as they passed before
The blind, but could not quite make out their talk
For noise in the room—the sudden heavy fall
And roll of a charred log, and the roused shower
Of snapping sparks; then sharply from the wall
The unforgivable crowing of the hour.
One instant set ajar, her quiet ear
Was stormed and forced by the full rout of day:
The rasp of a saw, the fussy cluck and bray
Of hens, the wheeze of a pump, she needs must hear;
She inescapably must endure to feel
Across her teeth the grinding of a backing wagon
    wheel.

IX

NOT over-kind nor over-quick in study
Nor skilled in sports nor beautiful was he.
He had come into her life when anybody
Would have been welcome, so in need was she.
They had become acquainted in this way:
He flashed a mirror in her eyes at school;
By which he was distinguished; from that day
They went about together, as a rule.
She told, in secret and with whispering,
How he had flashed a mirror in her eyes;
And as she told, it struck her with surprise
That this was not so wonderful a thing.
But what's the odds?—It's pretty nice to know
You've got a friend to keep you company everywhere
    you go.

X

SHE had forgotten how the August night
Was level as a lake beneath the moon,
In which she swam a little, losing sight
Of shore; and how the boy, that was at noon
Simple enough, not different from the rest,
Wore now a pleasant mystery as he went,
Which seemed to her an honest enough test
Whether she loved him, and she was content.
So loud, so loud the million crickets' choir . . .
So sweet the night, so long-drawn-out and late . . .
And if the man were not her spirit's mate,
Why was her body sluggish with desire?
Stark on the open field the moonlight fell,
But the oak tree's shadow was deep and black and
 secret as a well.

XI

It came into her mind, seeing how the snow
Was gone, and the brown grass exposed again,
And clothes-pins, and an apron—long ago,
In some white storm that sifted through the pane
And sent her forth reluctantly at last
To gather in, before the line gave way,
Garments, board-stiff, that galloped on the blast
Clashing like angel armies in a fray,
An apron long ago in such a night
Blown down and buried in the deepening drift,
To lie till April thawed it back to sight,
Forgotten, quaint and novel as a gift—
It struck her, as she pulled and pried and tore,
That here was spring, and the whole year to be lived
    through once more.

XII

TENDERLY, in those times, as though she fed
An ailing child—with sturdy propping up
Of its small, feverish body in the bed,
And steadying of its hands about the cup—
She gave her husband of her body's strength,
Thinking of men, what helpless things they were,
Until he turned and fell asleep at length,
And stealthily stirred the night and spoke to her.
Familiar, at such moments, like a friend,
Whistled far off the long, mysterious train,
And she could see in her mind's vision plain
The magic World, where cities stood on end . . .
Remote from where she lay—and yet—between,
Save for something asleep beside her, only the window
  screen.

XIII

FROM the wan dream that was her waking day,
Wherein she journeyed, borne along the ground
Without her own volition in some way,
Or fleeing, motionless, with feet fast bound,
Or running silent through a silent house
Sharply remembered from an earlier dream,
Upstairs, down other stairs, fearful to rouse,
Regarding him, the wide and empty scream
Of a strange sleeper on a malignant bed,
And all the time not certain if it were
Herself so doing or some one like to her,
From this wan dream that was her daily bread,
Sometimes, at night, incredulous, she would wake—
A child, blowing bubbles that the chairs and carpet
    did not break!

XIV

SHE had a horror he would die at night.
And sometimes when the light began to fade
She could not keep from noticing how white
The birches looked—and then she would be afraid,
Even with a lamp, to go about the house
And lock the windows; and as night wore on
Toward morning, if a dog howled, or a mouse
Squeaked in the floor, long after it was gone
Her flesh would sit awry on her. By day
She would forget somewhat, and it would seem
A silly thing to go with just this dream
And get a neighbor to come at night and stay.
But it would strike her sometimes, making the tea:
She had kept that kettle boiling all night long, for
    company.

XV

THERE was upon the sill a pencil mark,
Vital with shadow when the sun stood still
At noon, but now, because the day was dark,
It was a pencil mark upon the sill.
And the mute clock, maintaining ever the same
Dead moment, blank and vacant of itself,
Was a pink shepherdess, a picture frame,
A shell marked Souvenir, there on the shelf.
Whence it occurred to her that *he* might be,
The mainspring being broken in his mind,
A clock himself, if one were so inclined,
That stood at twenty minutes after three—
The reason being for this, it might be said,
That things in death were neither clocks nor people,
        but only dead.

XVI

THE doctor asked her what she wanted done
With him, that could not lie there many days.
And she was shocked to see how life goes on
Even after death, in irritating ways;
And mused how if he had not died at all
'Twould have been easier—then there need not be
The stiff disorder of a funeral
Everywhere, and the hideous industry,
And crowds of people calling her by name
And questioning her, she'd never seen before,
But only watching by his bed once more
And sitting silent if a knocking came . . .
She said at length, feeling the doctor's eyes,
"I don't know what you do exactly when a person
    dies."

XVII

GAZING upon him now, severe and dead,
It seemed a curious thing that she had lain
Beside him many a night in that cold bed,
And that had been which would not be again.
From his desirous body the great heat
Was gone at last, it seemed, and the taut nerves
Loosened forever.   Formally the sheet
Set forth for her to-day those heavy curves
And lengths familiar as the bedroom door.
She was as one that enters, sly, and proud,
To where her husband speaks before a crowd,
And sees a man she never saw before—
The man who eats his victuals at her side,
Small, and absurd, and hers: for once, not hers, un-
   classified.

THE END